working with cardboard and paper

working
with cardboard
and paper

HARVEY WEISS

ADDISON-WESLEY

THE BEGINNING ARTIST'S LIBRARY

OTHER TITLES BY THE SAME AUTHOR IN

THE BEGINNING ARTIST'S LIBRARY

1. CLAY, WOOD AND WIRE
   an introduction to sculpture

2. PAPER, INK AND ROLLER
   beginning printmaking

3. PENCIL, PEN AND BRUSH
   drawing in many media

4. STICKS, SPOOLS AND FEATHERS
   varied craft projects

5. CERAMICS — FROM CLAY TO KILN
   an introduction to ceramics

6. PAINT, BRUSH AND PALETTE
   beginning painting

7. COLLAGE AND CONSTRUCTION
   an introduction

8. LENS AND SHUTTER
   an introduction to photography

9. HOW TO MAKE YOUR OWN MOVIES
   an introduction to filmmaking

10. CARVING
    how to carve wood and stone

 A Young Scott Book

Text Copyright © 1978 by Harvey Weiss
Illustrations Copyright © 1978 by Harvey Weiss
All Rights Reserved
Addison-Wesley Publishing Company, Inc.
Reading, Massachusetts 01867
Printed in the United States of America
   CDEFGHIJK-WZ-79

Library of Congress Cataloging in Publication Data

Weiss, Harvey.
   Working with cardboard and paper.

   (The Beginning artist's library)
   SUMMARY: Instructions for projects made from cardboard and paper. Includes houses, castles, airplanes,
boats, and mobiles.

   1. Paper work — Juvenile literature.   2. Paperboard —
Juvenile literature.   [1. Paper work.   2. Paperboard.
3. Handicraft]   I. Title.
TT870.W425   745.54   77-21860
ISBN 0-201-09342-1

The models illustrated were made by the author
with the following exceptions:
page 6 by Christopher Barten,
page 17 by Daniel Rothenberg and
page 26 by Phillip Gibson.

CONTENTS

Introduction 7
1. Cardboard and Paper 9
2. Houses and Castles..16
3. Cardboard Airplanes..26
4. Cars, Boats, Trains 32
5. Cardboard Sculpture..40
6. All Kinds of Boxes 49
7. Cutouts and Cut Ups..52
8. Geometric Shapes...59
9. How to Make Your Own Paper...68

INTRODUCTION

Some of the most interesting and beautiful creations are made from very ordinary materials. A great cathedral is built with brick, stone and wood. A splendid statue can be fashioned out of common clay dug out of the earth. Ordinary plants, roots or dirt are mixed with oil to make the colors in the most elegant paintings. A noble work doesn't require noble materials!

As the illustrations on these pages show, materials as plain and ordinary as paper and cardboard can be used to make a great variety of worthwhile, handsome objects.

Cardboard and paper are flat — two dimensional. In some ways this is an advantage. In other ways it is a challenge. Sometimes it is a drawback. For example, if you want to make a flat design using different color papers, it is a simple matter to cut out the shapes you want and then just paste them down. If, on the other hand, you want to build a model of a house or boat, you will have to cut and shape and bend with planning and care.

There are all kinds of possibilities with cardboard and paper. You can cut and fold a sheet of cardboard to make a box strong enough to stand on. Or paper can be cut and shaped to make a delicate, lacy design that will flutter in the slightest breeze. You can make realistic animals, models, people. And it is possible to make all kinds of free-standing or hanging designs and constructions.

Another nice thing about this material is that it is cheap and plentiful. So it is easy to experiment and try out all kinds of ideas without worrying about wasting expensive materials. If you start something and it seems to be running into trouble or is turning out poorly, just toss it away and start again. Change your ideas and do it a different way.

The first part of this book is mostly about projects that use cardboard. The latter part is concerned with the possibilities of paper. However there is a great variety of cardboards and papers. Sometimes it is hard to tell the difference between a very heavy paper and a lightweight cardboard. So you will have to use your common sense and judgment in choosing the projects which are suitable for the materials you have to work with.

1. CARDBOARD AND PAPER

What is it?

Most paper is made from ground-up wood pulp. This material contains the cellulose fibers which are the main ingredient in paper — as well as cardboard. The wood pulp is ground up, treated in various chemical ways, mixed with water, then rolled out into sheets. (Chapter 9 discusses in greater detail the paper-making process and explains how you can make your own paper.)

There are many kinds of paper. There is very thin tissue paper, transparent tracing paper, heavy brown wrapping paper, blotting paper, paper in all colors like construction paper, and a great many other types designed for a particular purpose. Some of the constructions in this book can use any kind of paper. Some, like the geometric shape construction, need a fairly stiff, good quality paper. The kind of paper or cardboard needed for a particular project is discussed at the beginning of each chapter.

Cardboard is actually the same thing as paper. It is only thicker and stiffer and usually grey in color. The kind you use has a good deal to do with the sort of work that can be done, so it is discussed here in some detail.

Different Kinds of Cardboard

Shirt Cardboard

This is the kind that is found inside a shirt that has been sent to the laundry. It is fairly stiff and strong and is suitable for the types of construction discussed on these pages.

10

Package Cardboard

Cardboard is used in boxes and cartons of all kinds. A shoe box is a good example. This kind of cardboard often has one surface covered with a smooth paper which has been printed on. Occasionally the printed side can be used to good advantage if the colors are pleasant and the design can be made to fit in with what you are making. Because containers of this sort are already formed into neat, right-angled box shapes, you can sometimes save yourself a little work. You can use parts of these boxes, cut to the size you need.

Chip Board

This, too, is cardboard — only heavier and stiffer. You'll find it on the backs of large drawing pads and in cigar boxes. It is also used inside the covers of hard-bound books. You may find it difficult to locate this kind of cardboard. So, if you want to use something heavier than the two kinds listed above, you might have to go to an art or stationery store and buy some chip board. It comes in different weights. The heavier kind is too heavy. A piece of the lighter-weight chip board about 30 inches by 40 inches will cost about a dollar — not cheap for a piece of cardboard — but it will provide material for many projects.

Other Kinds

Once you start searching around for cardboard you'll find that there are quite a few varieties, different in weight, stiffness and texture. If you go to an art or stationery store, the variety will be even more extensive, if not confusing. A good art store will have chip board in two or more weights as well as illustration board, bristol board, mat board, mounting board, display board and so on. As long as the material is not thin and flexible and yet can be cut without too much trouble, you can use it.

Corrugated board is something quite different from cardboard. It is actually two layers of brown paper with a middle section that is rippled or wave-like. It is fine for certain kinds of large boxes or shipping containers. But it is not a very pleasant or easy material to use, and it isn't really suitable for most of the projects described in this book. The edges of corrugated board usually look ragged and unfinished. It is hard to fasten two pieces together, difficult to bend and has a slightly bumpy surface which is sometimes a bother. However it can be used for some kinds of large-scale constructions.

The Grain of Cardboard

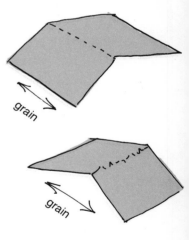

Surprising as it may seem, cardboard does have a grain, just as wood does. You can tell by cutting off a small square about 2 inches by 2 inches and folding it once up and down, and then once across from side to side. Compare the two creases. One will be neater and straighter than the other. The neat crease is the one that runs with the grain. The one that is irregular and bumpy will be across the grain.

Most of the time the direction of the grain doesn't have any importance at all — you can ignore the matter entirely. But in a few cases it is worth considering. For example, the round tower on the right should have the grain running up and down. This will make the rounded shape easier to bend. Or in the case of the airplane wings on page 28 the grain should run from tip to tip. This way the wings will be stiffer.

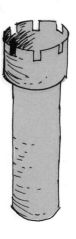

12

Cutting Cardboard

The thinner kinds of cardboard that come in a laundered shirt or a shoe box can be easily cut with a pair of sturdy, sharp scissors. But the heavier cardboards must be cut with a sharp knife like one of those shown below. A knife will also make a straighter cut and is needed for things like windows or doors.

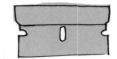

A single-edge razor blade will also cut cardboard quite neatly, but it must be used with care.

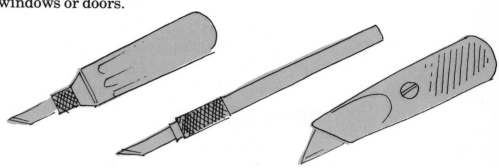

If you are careful, you can make an accurate cut, following a ruled line. (Be very careful to keep your hand behind the blade!) But you will get a straighter cut if you use a ruler to guide the blade. You must use a steel or aluminum ruler however. Wood is no good because the blade will snag into it. The ruler is held down firmly in place with one hand; the knife in the other. Be sure the ruler doesn't slip. You must do this kind of cutting with great care because you don't want the knife to hop off the cardboard, onto the ruler and into your hand! Observe these rules: 1. Don't press too hard. You don't have to cut through the board with one pass. The knife should be pulled over the cardboard several times until the blade goes through. 2. Don't

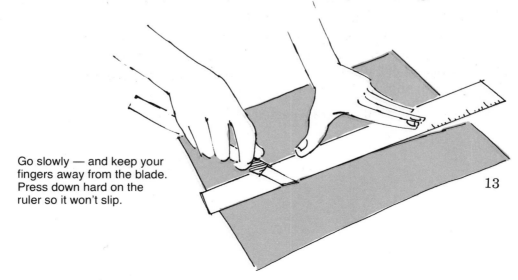

Go slowly — and keep your fingers away from the blade. Press down hard on the ruler so it won't slip.

13

pull the knife rapidly. Slow and easy does it. 3. Have a steady, flat surface to work on and a good light to see what you're doing. Place a piece of scrap cardboard or wood underneath your work. 4. Use a knife that is sharp! A dull blade which can slip about is more dangerous than a really sharp one. 5. Keep your fingers as far away from the edge of the ruler as possible.

The first few times you cut this way you may find that the knife blade wanders away from the edge of the ruler. But with a little practice it is an easy matter to keep the knife against the ruler as you move it along.

Bending Cardboard

If you want to get a sharp, neat, accurate bend in cardboard, you must first score it. That means running a *dull* knife blade along the line where the fold is to be. A butter knife or paper clip will work well, and a ruler should be used as a guide. If you are using very thin cardboard or very heavy paper, a finger nail will do the trick. The score is made along the inside of the bend.

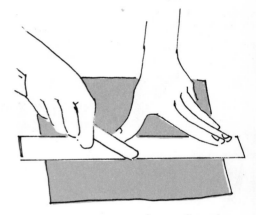

scoring cardboard

When you are using a heavier cardboard the scoring is done somewhat differently. In this case a sharp knife is used, and the score is made along the *outside* of the bend. The knife is pressed down hard enough to cut through the surface of the cardboard. The thicker the cardboard the deeper the cut. Be careful not to cut all the way through.

When you want to make a gentle, curved bend in cardboard it is a good idea to dampen it a little. And the bend should be made with the grain. There is a limit, however, to how far you can bend cardboard before it will crack. Some stiff cardboard can hardly be bent at all. In this case, many scores, close together, will have to be made, and you will get your bend by means of a series of sharp bends.

14

Joining Cardboard

One of the problems in working with cardboard is how to attach one piece to another. When one surface is to be placed flat on top of another a dab of glue will do the job easily. But when you want to join an edge of one piece to the edge of another, it is not always easy to get a strong attachment. Some of the different methods for joining cardboard are shown below. A white glue like Elmer's is the best type for our purposes. It is strong and fast drying.

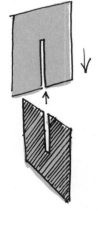

If narrow slits are cut in two pieces of cardboard, they can be fitted together quite neatly and fairly rigidly.

To get a neat slit, make two cuts very close together. Then remove the little sliver of cardboard remaining between the cuts.

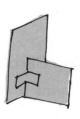
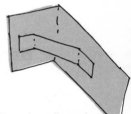

A small tab or flap of cardboard will strengthen a corner.

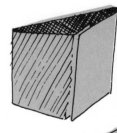

If the end of a piece of cardboard is scored, then folded, a large gluing surface is created.

A small block of wood glued into the corner, where two pieces of cardboard join, will make a strong joint.

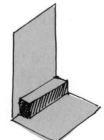

The strongest attachment is made when one flat surface is glued right down onto another.

When the cardboard edge is perfectly straight it can be glued onto a flat surface. However, this is not the strongest kind of attachment.

Sometimes staples can be used, although they aren't very neat to look at.

2. HOUSES AND CASTLES

Cardboard is the ideal material for making models of all kinds of buildings. What the carpenter and mason do with great skill and effort, you can do — on a small scale — with scissors or knife and glue. Architects often build models of the buildings they are planning before actual work is started. It is one thing to look at a drawing or blueprint, and another to look at an actual three-dimensional object, even if it is only a small size version of the real thing.

You don't have to be an architect to make little houses, buildings, castles. (You can pretend you are and see how you like this as a profession.) These little houses are fun to make even if they have no practical use at all. You may, in fact, want to make a completely impractical or imaginary dwelling. You can make a very modern house, a fort, a museum for miniature treasures, a mouse house, a tree house. You can make a model of some famous structure like the White House, Monticello, Chartres Cathedral . . .

On the other hand, you might prefer to make a model of the house in which you live — or would like to live in one day.

17

If you want to make a model of a house that already exists or that you would like to build, it should be in scale. That means that all the sizes in your model should be in proportion to the full size house. For example, suppose your real house measures 20 feet by 24 feet and the roof is 14 feet high. If you make a model of this house with a scale of 1 foot equals 1 inch, the model would measure 20 inches by 24 inches and the roof would be 14 inches high. This would be a large model. Suppose you make your model to a scale of 1 foot equals ½ inch. Now the model would measure 10 inches by 12 inches with the roof 7 inches high.

This entire business of scale is only important when you want to make an accurate model of something that exists or will be built from the model. Otherwise just forget all about all this and simply build what looks right to you.

The description that follows is for the plain and simple kind of house. There is really no reason you have to follow the sizes and proportions given. You may prefer something quite different. However, the step-by-step procedure given should be understood because it can be used with almost any type of house, barn, shed, train station or whatever has four walls and a roof.

1. First, measure out the four walls. It is important that these measurements be accurate if you want your model to stand up straight with an even top and bottom and all edges parallel.

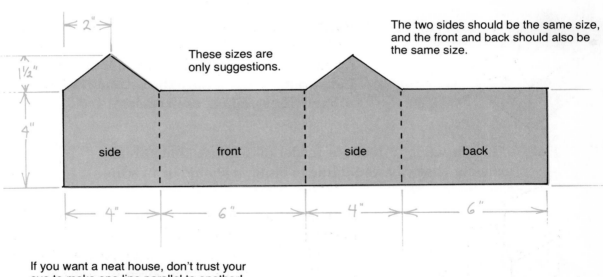

These sizes are only suggestions.

The two sides should be the same size, and the front and back should also be the same size.

| 2" |
| 1½" |
| 4" |

side   front   side   back

4"   6"   4"   6"

If you want a neat house, don't trust your eye to make one line parallel to another! Measure up the same distance in two places from the edge of your cardboard. Then draw a line with a ruler between the two marks. This line will then be parallel with the edge. You can use the same method — measuring in from the side edge of the cardboard — to get up and down lines (vertical) that are parallel to the side of the cardboard.

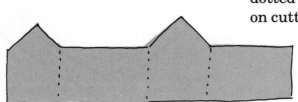

2. Cut out the walls and then score along the dotted lines. (Be sure to read the previous chapter on cutting and scoring.)

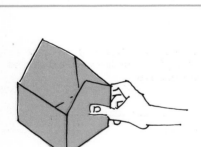

3. Next, draw in the window and door. If you want to have actual cutouts, now is the time to do it, while the walls can still be laid down flat. (Be sure you have a sharp knife for this.)

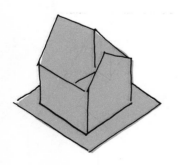

4. Apply glue to the edges and assemble the walls. Press the edges together until the glue has dried enough to hold. Stand the four walls on a flat surface to make sure the bottoms are even all around. If not, adjust as necessary.

5. Cut out a base that is slightly larger than the house. This will provide a lot of extra strength and stiffness. Glue the bottom of the walls onto this. (If you plan to add a porch or steps or anything else, leave room for these additions.)

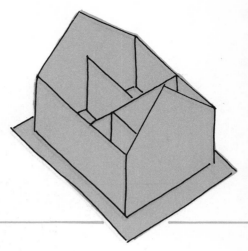

6. If you are going to make interior walls, do it now. Measure and cut accurately so that they will fit snugly. If the fit is a little bit off, use small tabs or blocks of wood for support.

7. The roof is made from one large piece of cardboard, scored and folded at the peak. Don't glue the roof down if you want to be able to remove it and look inside the model.

Allow a little extra cardboard for an overhang on ends and sides.

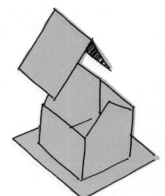

8. The chimney is a small box with a notch cut out of the bottom of opposite sides.

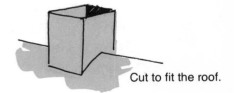

Cut to fit the roof.

9. The amount of extra detail you want to add is up to you. If you want to take the time, there are a great many little additions that will make the model more realistic. You can add things like front steps, a porch, dormer windows, a TV antenna on the chimney, stripping around the windows and doors, and so on. You can also paint the house if you feel like it.

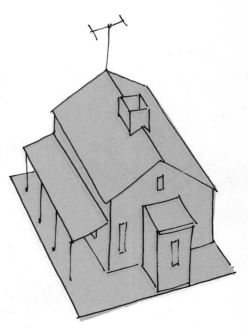

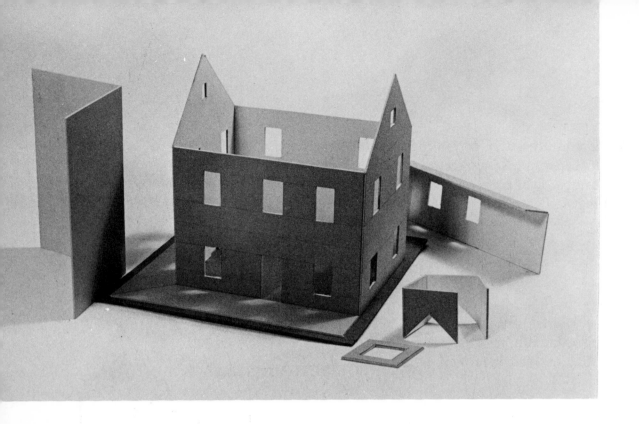

Some Odd and Fanciful Houses

All buildings aren't practical or conventional, and it can be great fun to experiment with unusual types of construction and off-beat forms. There is no reason why you have to be a "purist" and stick to cardboard alone. As in the models shown here, sticks, string, plastic and various other materials can be used along with the cardboard.

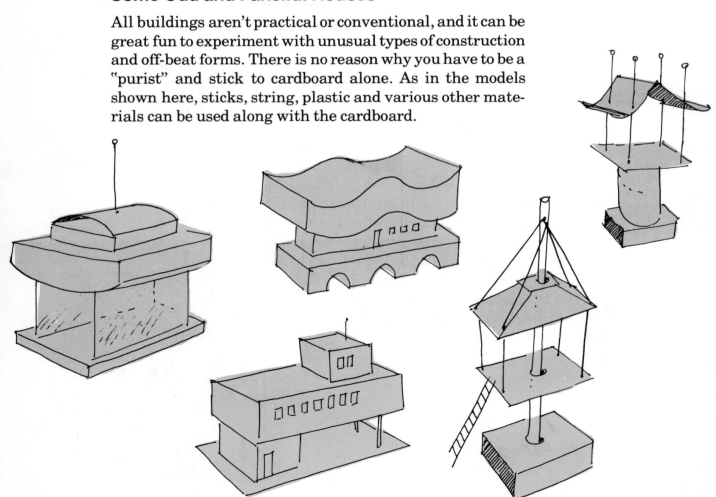

The outside wall is removed to show the interior.

Remember to cut all doors and windows while the cardboard is still flat and easy to work on.

A Mouse House

This is a fine dwelling for a pet mouse, guinea pig, gerbil or any other small creature you may happen to own.

Castles

A castle is no more difficult to put together than the small house already described. The only difference is that the castle has more parts and is built in a different style.

A round tower can be made from the round cardboard cylinders on which aluminum foil, waxed paper or toilet paper are wrapped.

The little notches along the upper walls of many castles are called "crenelations". They served to protect the defending soldiers from enemy missiles.

Several individual parts can be joined together to make the complete castle. And it can be as large and elaborate as you choose.

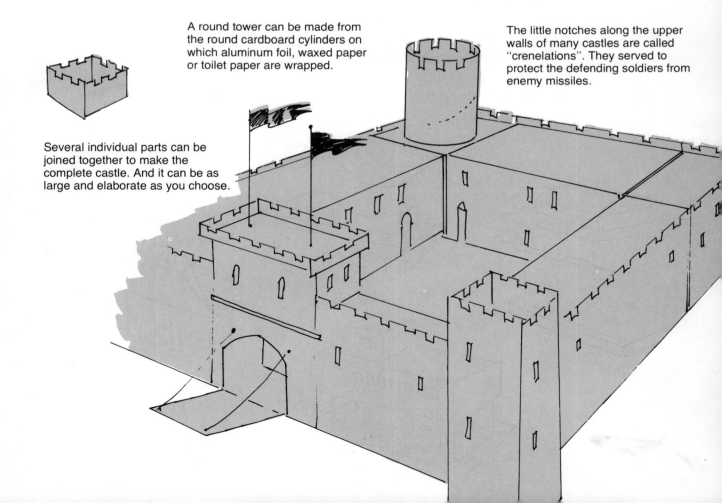

The Whole Town!

A large, intricate model like this may seem at first glance a very difficult undertaking. It isn't. It is simply a combination of many small parts, and practically all the parts are plain box shapes, like the simple house described earlier. Some of the shapes are tall. Some have windows and doors. One has a skylight. The only tricky operation is in the cutting of the curved top of doors and windows. This must be done carefully. A line drawn with a compass or bottle top is needed as a guide. Mat board, obtained from an art store, should be used instead of plain gray cardboard. This kind of board is white on one side and colored on the other. When this kind of board is scored (cut into) with a knife and then bent, some of the inner material can be seen. This appears as a white line that contrasts with the colored surface of the board. It makes a nice accent.

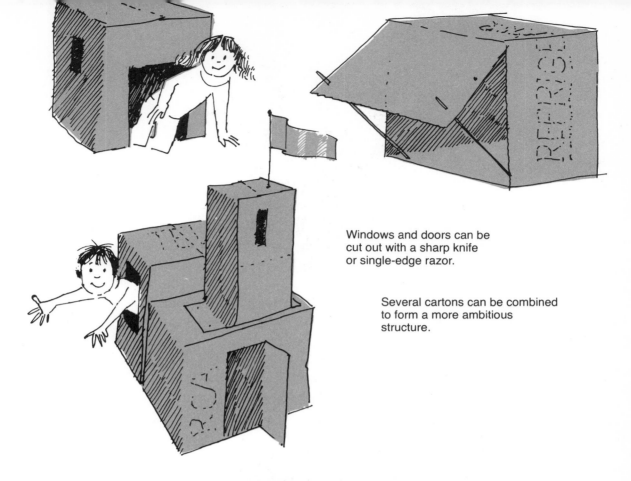

Windows and doors can be
cut out with a sharp knife
or single-edge razor.

Several cartons can be combined
to form a more ambitious
structure.

Using Corrugated Board

The houses and castles discussed so far have been fairly
small. But there are also ways of working with much
larger forms.

The best material for large constructions is corrugated
board. If you can collect a few large cartons, you'll have the
material for some quite ambitious structures. You can
often get suitable cartons from stores that sell bedding and
mattresses, refrigerators, television sets, furniture. This
sort of merchandise is shipped by the manufacturer in
large corrugated packages which are discarded by the
stores. You can usually have them just for the asking.

The drawings above show a few ways this material can
be used to build structures large enough to get inside of.

25

3. CARDBOARD AIRPLANES

When most people think of model airplanes they think of balsa wood or plastic or pine. These are the usual materials out of which models are made. But cardboard is also a perfectly practical material. Cardboard models, like the ones shown here, may not be quite as rugged as some others. But their great advantage is that they can be put together speedily, and because cardboard is plentiful, it is easy to try out different designs without a lot of elaborate planning.

The directions that follow show how a World War I bi-plane can be put together. This method of construction is the same as for many other types of planes. So, if you would rather build a different plane, simply change the proportions and placement of parts to get what you want.

The only tricky part in building the bi-plane is the attachment of the upper wing and landing gear. Thin strips of cardboard can be used for this. But you will get a sturdier aircraft if you use a few small sticks. Thin dowels, about ⅛ inch diameter, will work fine. Lollipop sticks will work well, or you can snip off small straight twigs from any tree or bush that isn't too soft or flexible. Thin strips of bamboo, coat hanger wire, paper clip wire or any thin, stiff material can be used.

1. The fuselage is made from one piece of cardboard. The dotted lines are where you score and fold. Measure accurately.

Adjust the dimensions to suit the sort of plane you want to build. If you don't like the shape of your first attempt, junk it and start again!

The grain of the cardboard should be running the long way as you want a neat fold.

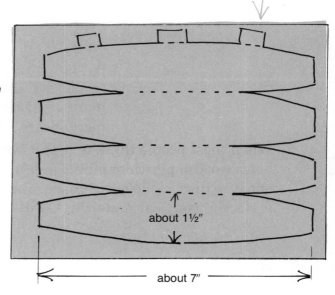

tab

about 1½"

about 7"

2. Cut along the lines you've drawn. Then score (see page 14) along the dotted lines.

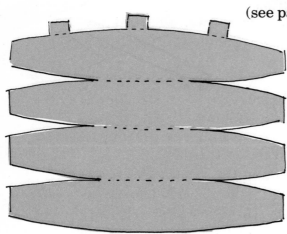

3. Apply glue to the tabs, then bend into position. Use a few rubber bands to hold everything in place until the glue dries. If there are any gaps, smear on a little more glue and hold the edges together until the glue holds.

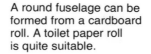

A round fuselage can be formed from a cardboard roll. A toilet paper roll is quite suitable.

4. The wings can be made out of a single strip of cardboard. But they will be a little stronger and more realistic looking if you cut out a double piece. Score and fold it as shown. Glue down the edges. If you don't bend over the leading edge too sharply, the wing can be given a little thickness.

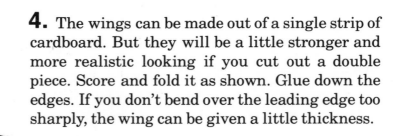

5. Both wings are made the same way, but the top one has a scoop cut out of the trailing edge. Glue the lower wing to the bottom of the fuselage.

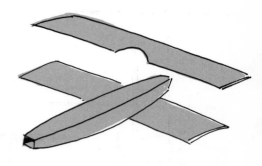

Most bi-planes have a little scoop cut out of the upper wing to improve visibility for the pilot.

6. The upper wing is attached in any of the ways shown below. If you can find some sticks, you can poke small holes and then run the sticks right through the fuselage, letting them project through the bottom to support the wheels.

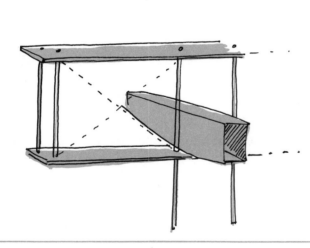

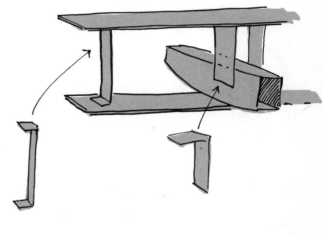

7. Make the wheels from two or three circles of cardboard, glued together. When the glue has dried, round and smooth the edges with sandpaper. Paint the edges black, and you will have what looks like rubber tires.

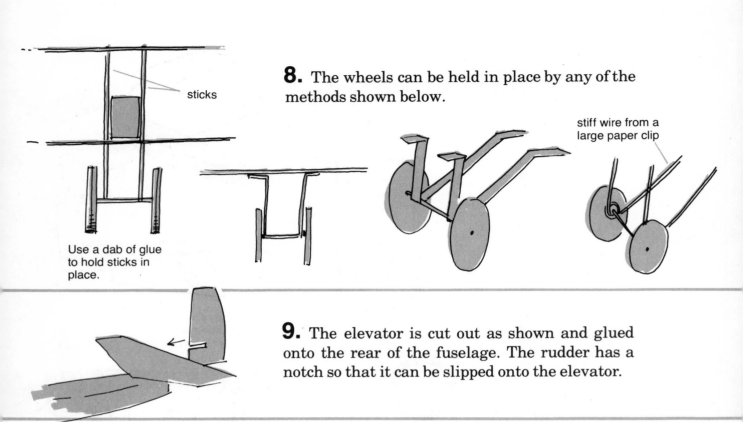

sticks

Use a dab of glue to hold sticks in place.

8. The wheels can be held in place by any of the methods shown below.

stiff wire from a large paper clip

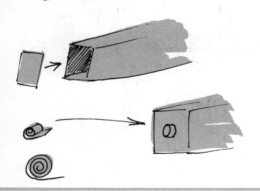

9. The elevator is cut out as shown and glued onto the rear of the fuselage. The rudder has a notch so that it can be slipped onto the elevator.

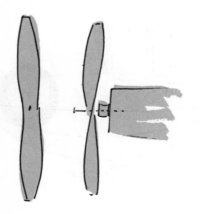

10. Cut out and glue a small piece of cardboard over the front end of the fuselage. A hub for the propeller is made from a thin strip of cardboard that has been dampened, smeared with glue, then rolled up tight.

11. The propeller is cut out as shown, dampened and given a twist. Put a pin through the center and into the hub, and the propeller will be able to spin about.

12. A pilot can be cut out of a scrap of cardboard. Paint him as shown, stick a piece of wool yarn under his nose for a moustache, and you will have a very fierce-looking aviator.

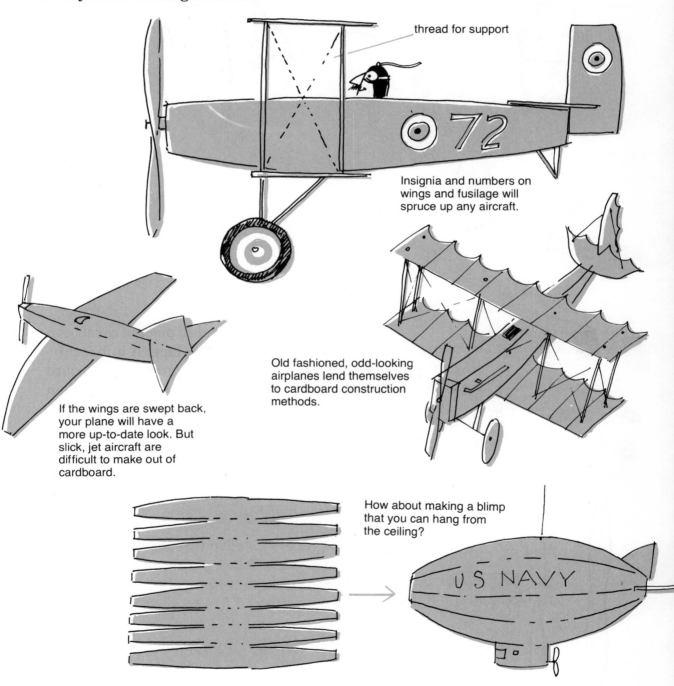

thread for support

Insignia and numbers on wings and fusilage will spruce up any aircraft.

If the wings are swept back, your plane will have a more up-to-date look. But slick, jet aircraft are difficult to make out of cardboard.

Old fashioned, odd-looking airplanes lend themselves to cardboard construction methods.

How about making a blimp that you can hang from the ceiling?

U S NAVY

4. CARS, BOATS, TRAINS

The models in this chapter are built with the same material and using the same methods as were used to build the cardboard airplane in the previous chapter. It is possible to make models of this sort that are very realistic. You can refer to drawings and photographs in reference books. Be very careful and accurate. And it is also possible to be unrealistic and fanciful using shapes and proportions that are exaggerated and humorous. You must decide for yourself which approach to take.

An Old Fashioned Racing Car

The kind of car shown here is typical of the ones that competed around 1910 in America and in Europe. They

32

usually had two seats — one for the driver and one for the mechanic — and they reached speeds of well over 100 miles per hour. When this type of car wasn't used in racing but as a run-about, it usually had fenders and a running board.

1. Make the chassis first. This is a simple rectangle, and it is the "spine" of your car. It should be fairly stiff, so cut out two pieces of cardboard the same size and glue them together. (The sizes shown in the drawings are only suggestions. You may want to make a larger or smaller model.)

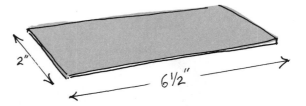

2"

6½"

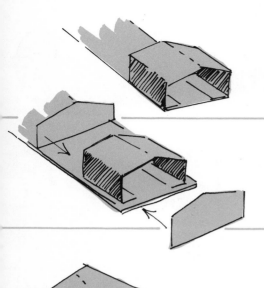

2. The hood is made like a small house with a peaked roof. Glue it onto the chassis.

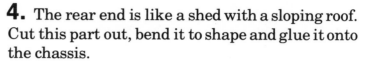

3. Next cut out the radiator and glue it to the front of the hood. Another piece of cardboard is glued to the back.

4. The rear end is like a shed with a sloping roof. Cut this part out, bend it to shape and glue it onto the chassis.

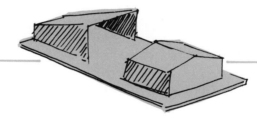

seat

5. The seat is made in two parts. First the seat, then two pieces along the sides.

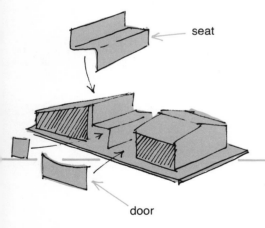

door

6. The wheels are the trickiest part of this model. They make the difference between a good-looking racer and a sloppy-looking one, so take your time and do a neat job.

Two or three round pieces of cardboard glued together will make a sturdy wheel.

The wheels on the model shown in the photograph on page 32 have a round cardboard circle which is glued to a thin slice cut from a cardboard tube. The spokes are thin sticks. Wooden match-sticks or toothpicks can be used for this.

7. The wheels are held in place by means of a pencil axle. Cut off the point and eraser end of a pencil so that it is about ¼ inch wider than the chassis. Scrape the paint off one side (so the glue will stick better) and glue it to the underside of the chassis.

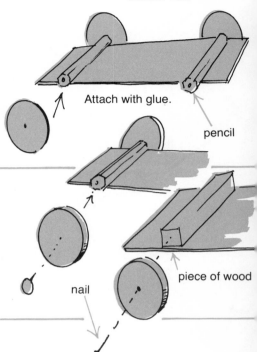

bottom view

Attach with glue.

pencil

8. Glue the wheels to the ends of the pencil. With this arrangement the wheels won't turn, which is all right for a model that is intended only for display. If you want the wheels to turn, you will have to use one of the methods shown.

nail

piece of wood

9. The fenders and running board are cut out of one strip of cardboard. They are held in place with little tabs.

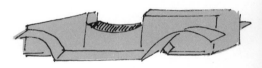

10. The windshield, steering wheel, headlights and other little details will add a great deal of interest to the finished model. A fancy paint job will also do much to dress it up.

A little cardboard circle glued to a thin stick will make the steering wheel.

A paper clip will make the windshield.

Make an ornament for the hood!

spare tire

headlights

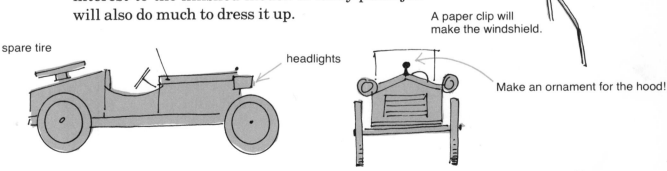

35

A Tugboat

A cardboard boat is simpler to make than might at first appear. Once the large piece for the hull is made, the other steps follow logically.

It is a simple matter to change the shapes and proportions of the model shown here to get other types of boats. An ocean liner, an aircraft carrier or a sailboat can be made by altering the hull shape and the superstructure.

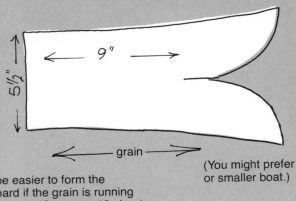

Cut out this shape to form the hull. Gently bend up along the center and glue the front edge together. You will probably have to hold it with your fingers until the glue sets. The rear part of the hull is temporarily held in position by several rubber bands.

(You might prefer a larger or smaller boat.)

Glue this edge together.

It will be easier to form the cardboard if the grain is running the long way. (See page 12 about the grain of cardboard.)

The deck is glued down on top of the hull. Don't bother to cut it to the exact shape. Attach the approximate shape, and after the glue has dried you can cut off the excess with a very sharp knife or a single-edge razor blade.

Get a smooth, rounded shape with no creases or sharp bends.

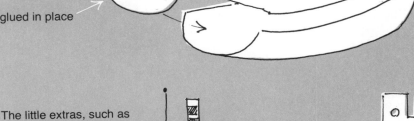

stern glued in place

The cabin is simply a little box or house with doors and portholes.

The little extras, such as smokestack, mast, radar antenna, etc., add a good deal of realism. A neat paint job will also look good.

If the finished model has a water-tight hull with no gaps or pin holes and has been given several coats of paint, it can be put in the water. However, if it is to float properly, it will need some ballast. That means that some weight in the form of nuts and bolts or pebbles must be placed inside the hull.

A cardboard stand will support the finished model and make it look more important.

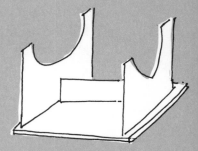

The method described here can be used to build many different kinds of boats. By changing the hull shape and superstructure, you can make anything from a sailing ship to an ocean liner or battleship.

A Steam Locomotive

This old fashioned locomotive is made up almost entirely of round shapes. The wheels, boiler, smokestack and many of the other parts are circular. The boiler is made from a cardboard tube from inside a roll of toilet paper. The smokestack and cylinders are made from tightly rolled up strips of cardboard.

38

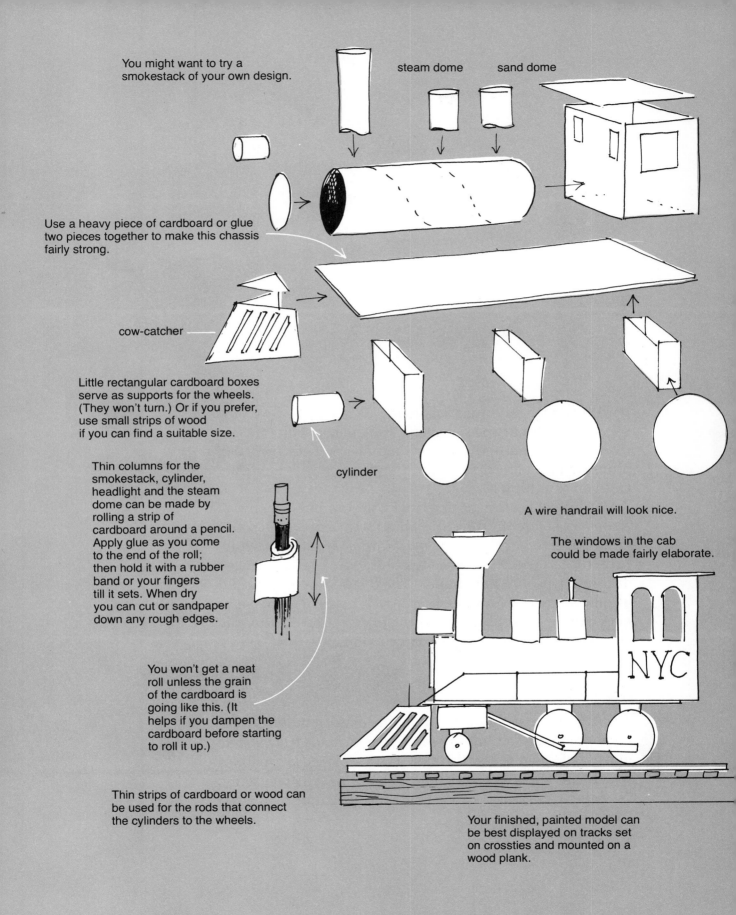

You might want to try a smokestack of your own design.

steam dome   sand dome

Use a heavy piece of cardboard or glue two pieces together to make this chassis fairly strong.

cow-catcher

Little rectangular cardboard boxes serve as supports for the wheels. (They won't turn.) Or if you prefer, use small strips of wood if you can find a suitable size.

cylinder

Thin columns for the smokestack, cylinder, headlight and the steam dome can be made by rolling a strip of cardboard around a pencil. Apply glue as you come to the end of the roll; then hold it with a rubber band or your fingers till it sets. When dry you can cut or sandpaper down any rough edges.

A wire handrail will look nice.

The windows in the cab could be made fairly elaborate.

You won't get a neat roll unless the grain of the cardboard is going like this. (It helps if you dampen the cardboard before starting to roll it up.)

NYC

Thin strips of cardboard or wood can be used for the rods that connect the cylinders to the wheels.

Your finished, painted model can be best displayed on tracks set on crossties and mounted on a wood plank.

5. CARDBOARD SCULPTURE

Until recently sculpture was modeled in clay or wax, or it was carved from wood or stone. But today sculptors use many new, sometimes unusual, materials. They use steel, aluminum, plastics, wire cloth and just about anything else you can think of.

Cardboard is often used to make preliminary studies of sculpture before the full scale work is started. Cardboard is not, of course, any good for very large, permanent sculpture. But it is perfectly fine for small, light-weight designs of thin forms and flat shapes. The flat sheets of steel and aluminum, which are much used today, are in many ways very similar to cardboard. Stiff paper can be used instead of cardboard for some of these constructions.

Stabiles

An American sculptor by the name of Alexander Calder gave the name "stabile" to sculpture he made from sheets of metal. Calder is also the man who developed the mobiles which are described on the following pages. The name "stabile" was used because this kind of sculpture is quite

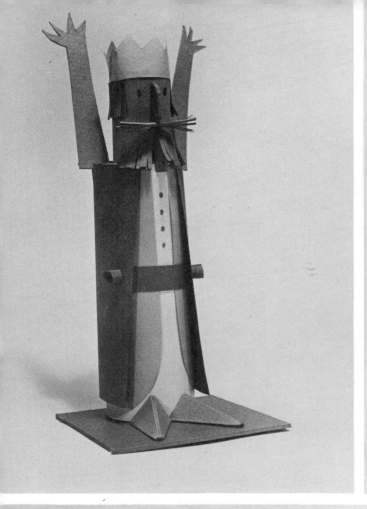

similar in many ways to mobiles — but they don't move. Something that stays in one place is a stabile.

A stabile is a combination of silhouettes. There are no volumes or solids as in most sculpture. Because of this, the design will change as you shift your point of view. What may appear as a large flat area will gradually change to a thin line as you move. This is one of the very interesting things about this kind of sculpture.

There is no one way or correct way to make a stabile. Some people will have an idea of what the finished design will look like before they start. They have a picture in their mind. Then all they do is put the picture into actual form.

Some people just have a vague idea about the kind of shapes they like — perhaps curved or jagged or squarish — and then cut out some shapes of this sort. When they have made a few pieces they will try combining them in various ways until they get an arrangement they like. Then some means of attaching them together is worked out.

Other people will simply pick up a piece of cardboard and scissors and start cutting. Most people begin to get ideas once they have the tools and materials in their hands and begin to work.

The drawings below and the photographs show a few different kinds of stabiles and the manner in which the different parts are joined. You'll probably find that in many cases a few slits in the cardboard will make the most simple and strong attachment.

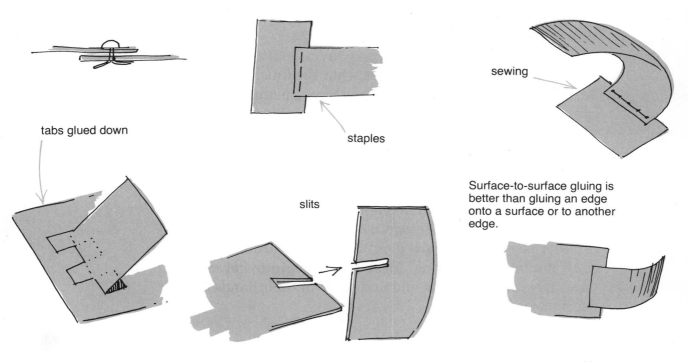

tabs glued down

staples

sewing

slits

Surface-to-surface gluing is better than gluing an edge onto a surface or to another edge.

43

Creatures and Critters

The photographs and drawings here show some of the more realistic — and not so realistic — kinds of sculpture you can get with cardboard. (You could also use a stiff paper for many of these designs.) In many ways these constructions are very similar to the stabiles. You are working with a series of silhouette, cut-out shapes. And in many cases the various parts are held together with interlocking slits.

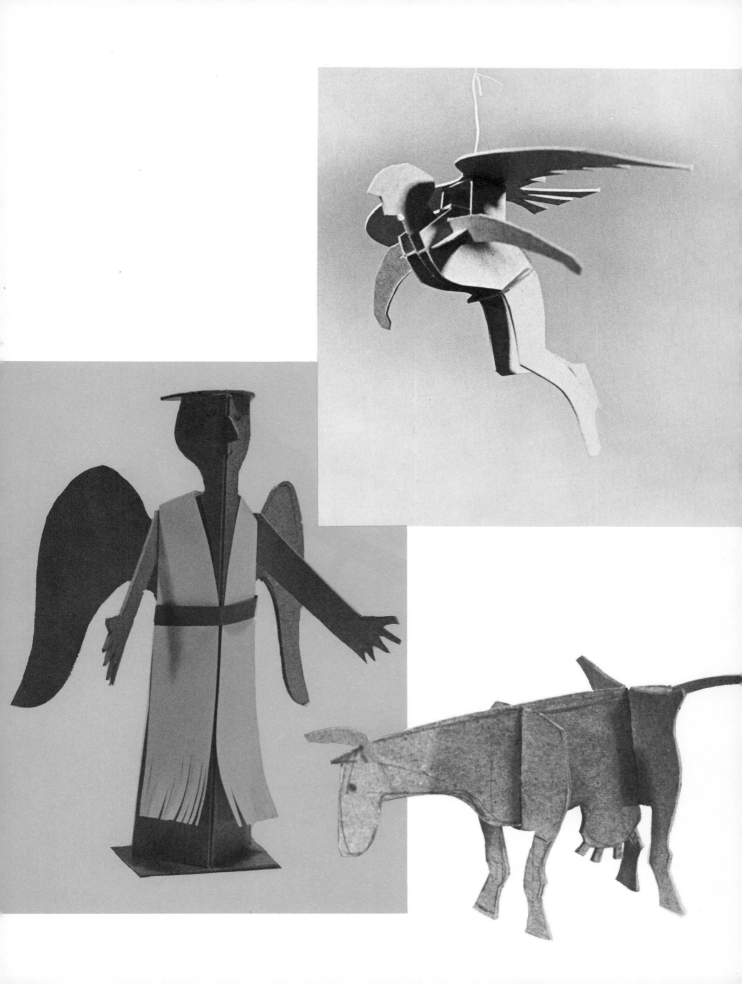

Mobiles

Any sculpture which is hung from the ceiling and which can move about as a draft or breeze strikes it is called a mobile. The thin, flat shape of cardboard lends itself to this kind of sculpture very readily. A mobile will turn and twist about, and the pattern and relationship of the parts will always be changing. The sculpture is never exactly the same. This is one of the nicest things about mobiles.

You will find that in most cases the mobiles you make will look best if you limit yourself to shapes of one type. For example, if you decide to make a mobile with curved forms, try to keep all of the forms somewhat curved. Or, if you are using angular forms, stick to that kind of shape. A certain unity is assured this way. And also be sure to remember that this rule — like all rules in art — should be broken if you disagree or have other ideas!

The following steps show the method for assembling a simple mobile:

1. A mobile is made from the bottom up. Cut out the first, or bottom piece, in the shape you want. Cut a thin slit. Fit a piece of thread. into the slit. It will probably stay in place by itself, but a drop of glue will make certain that it does.

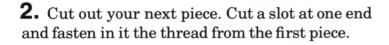

2. Cut out your next piece. Cut a slot at one end and fasten in it the thread from the first piece.

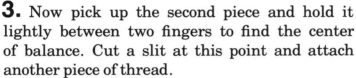

3. Now pick up the second piece and hold it lightly between two fingers to find the center of balance. Cut a slit at this point and attach another piece of thread.

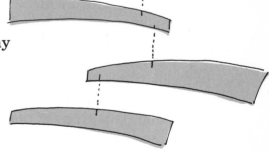

center of balance

4. This same procedure is repeated for as many pieces as you want.

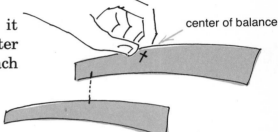

This is just one type of mobile. There are all sorts of other combinations of shapes and sizes that are possible. But, if you use the method of working from the bottom to the top, as explained here, you'll find that your design will move and balance well.

When you have finished your mobile, hang it up somewhere where it will cast a shadow. This is as much fun to watch as the mobile itself!

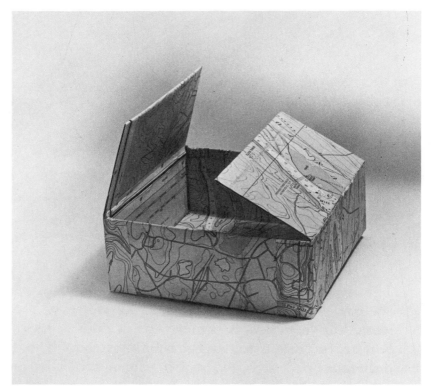

This box was covered with a marine chart. It would be a suitable container for some sea-going object, such as a compass or piece of navigation equipment. The box below has an interior dividing wall.

6. ALL KINDS OF BOXES

The model buildings in the first chapter and many parts of
the model planes and cars are box-like. However a box, by
itself, has six sides — the four vertical sides and a top and
bottom. So the construction is a bit more complicated. The
drawings below show the basic plan of most boxes. The four
sides are folded up, and the corners are glued together.
However, you don't get a joint that is as strong as you
might like if you attach cardboard edge to edge with glue.
So flaps are often added as shown in the drawing. These
give a much larger surface for the glue to stick to. The box
will be much stronger.

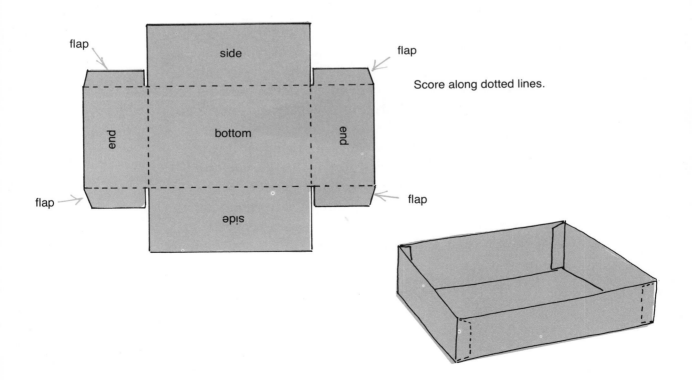

flap

flap

side

end

bottom

end

side

flap

flap

Score along dotted lines.

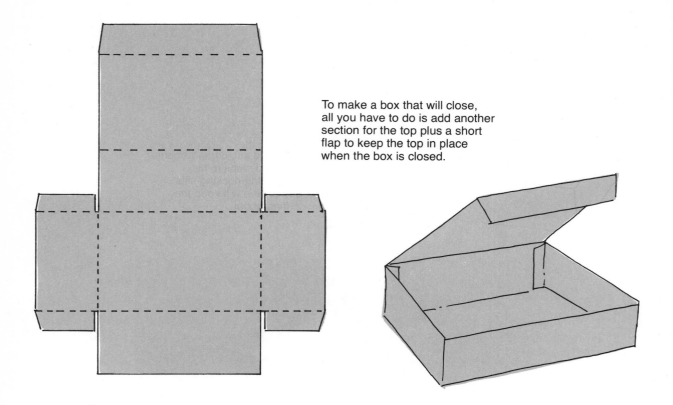

To make a box that will close, all you have to do is add another section for the top plus a short flap to keep the top in place when the box is closed.

The size of the box you make and the kind of cardboard you use will be determined by what you intend to put in it. A box to hold a delicate silk scarf or a butterfly doesn't have to be very rugged. But if you wanted some boxes to store and display a collection of rocks, you would need an entirely different kind of box.

If the box you make is to be strong and neat, you must take your time to measure carefully before you do any cutting and scoring. The lines you draw should be parallel or at right angles to one another, unless you are making a box in an odd shape.

A box can be a useful container for something, or it can be an interesting and amusing thing in itself. Various pasted-on coverings or inside linings can be used. Wallpaper in bright, colorful patterns or clippings from magazines work very well. Boxes of this sort can be very attractive if done with humor and imagination.

50

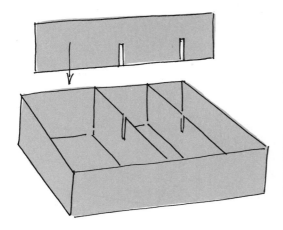

A box can be divided into compartments by making well-fitted strips to fit between the sides. Interlocking slits and a few dabs of glue will keep the strips from shifting about.

This narrow box was made to hold envelopes. The cardboard was covered with paper cut from a fancy shopping bag. The paper used to cover a box should be carefully cut to the proper size before it is glued down.

7. CUTOUTS AND CUT UPS

When a sheet of paper is folded up like an accordian and then wedges are cut out of the sides, you will get a pattern of diamond-shaped "windows" when the paper is opened up. This is the "cutting-out-paper-dolls" process which you have, no doubt, tried at one time or another.

Even though this is the simplest of methods, it is possible to get some very elegant designs if you cut out shapes that are varied instead of plain triangles or squares.

The design can be varied not only by the kind of shapes you cut out, but by the way the paper is folded.

The way the paper is folded, as well as the kind of shapes cut out of it, will determine the sort of pattern you will end up with. Experiment with as many different possibilities as you can think of.

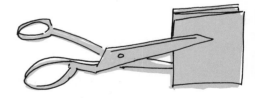

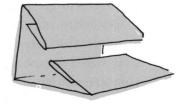

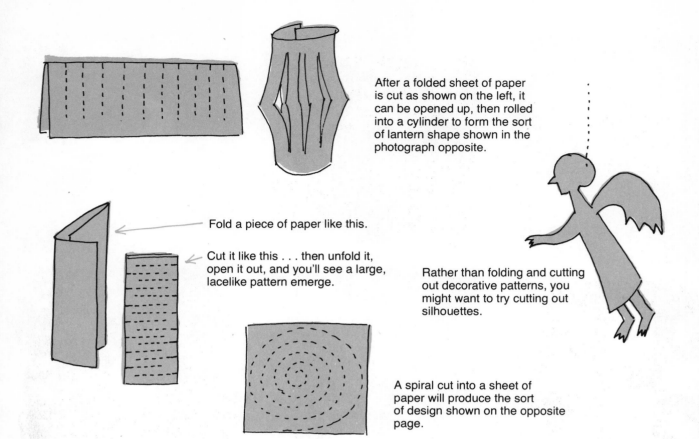

After a folded sheet of paper is cut as shown on the left, it can be opened up, then rolled into a cylinder to form the sort of lantern shape shown in the photograph opposite.

Fold a piece of paper like this.

Cut it like this . . . then unfold it, open it out, and you'll see a large, lacelike pattern emerge.

Rather than folding and cutting out decorative patterns, you might want to try cutting out silhouettes.

A spiral cut into a sheet of paper will produce the sort of design shown on the opposite page.

Most cutouts are rather flimsy, especially if you have used a light weight paper. In order to give them a little more permanence they can be pasted down on another piece of paper of a different color. The colored background will make the cutout pattern stand out much more clearly and will keep a delicate design from getting ripped accidentally.

If you want to cover a large space or make a wall hanging or mural, get a large sheet of paper. Or join several pieces together. Then paste down a variety of cutout patterns in different colors. That is the way the design at the top of the previous page was made.

Cutout patterns don't have to be flat. There are ways of cutting the paper so that it can be formed into large, expanded shapes. Some of the different methods of doing this are shown below.

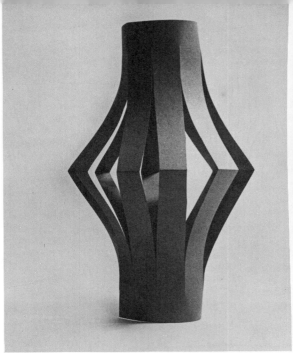

Paper Mosaics

The traditional way of making a mosaic is with small pieces of colored marble, ceramic or glass. These materials are imbedded in cement to form a permanent, strong surface for walls or floors. There are mosaics in existence today that were made thousands of years ago.

It is possible to get the same effects as in these traditional mosaics using paper. Different colored papers can be cut into small pieces and pasted down to get some very elegant designs.

You should have no trouble getting a wide variety of colors. A few old magazines will provide a good supply. Rip out the pages that have a lot of color. Even if the color is part of some photograph or drawing, it can be used. For example, the hair of a model in a shampoo ad might give you a nice yellow-brown. Once this area has been cut up you won't know it is hair. All you will see is the color. Colors can also be found in gift-wrapping paper, shopping bags, leftover pieces of wallpaper and various kinds of packages. Or you can use a package of multi-colored construction paper. This will combine well with all the other colors you may find.

This is how to proceed:

Make a rough drawing on a piece of paper or cardboard. Don't worry about making something neat or very well drawn. As you work you will no doubt make all kinds of changes and perhaps even end up with something completely different from what you started out to make.

Cut your paper into thin strips. Then, you can cut out the shapes you want as you need them. The traditional mosaic tile is a small rectangle about ⅜ inch wide and ½ inch long. You may want to keep this as the basic shape and size of your paper "tile," or you may choose to use a larger or smaller tile. You can use quite large pieces of paper cut in various shapes. This can look very nice. But it won't have the quality of a mosaic. A mosaic is made up of many *small* pieces.

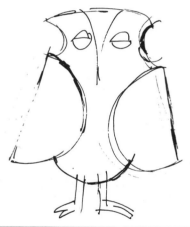

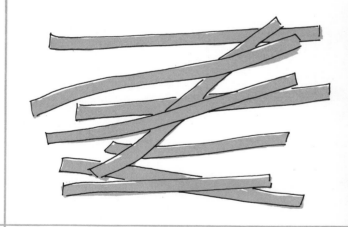

The paper tile is fastened down with paste. Use a small brush spreading it over the entire back of the tile. If you use just a small dab, the chances are that the corners will curl up, and this will look sloppy. Use a pair of tweezers and work on a sheet of newspaper, or your hands and the front of the tiles will be a mess in no time at all.

One of the nice things about mosaics is that you get patterns from the tiles. By placing them in rows, or curves or square blocks you can get some very interesting effects. You may, in fact, decide you want to concentrate on these patterns and not even bother with any realistic subjects.

Paper strips can be used for weavings like these. If construction paper in interesting colors is used, the results will be very attractive. The pattern on the right was formed by using curved strips.

58

8. GEOMETRIC SHAPES

The geometric shapes shown here are handsome things which make lovely decorations. But they are also rather surprising objects because they are so firm and solid — which is not the nature of paper. It is probably this change from a floppy, loose sheet of paper into a firm geometric shape that people find so fascinating.

The construction of these shapes is not difficult if you go carefully step by step. The first time you make one of these shapes is the hardest. After that it will go fast. Almost any kind of paper is suitable as long as it is not tissue thin nor cardboard hard.

A Polyhedron

This is a shape with many triangular planes. It is quite amazing that a shape this complicated can be made from one sheet of paper. Here's how it is done:

1. Cut a sheet of paper into a square. About 8 inches on each side is a good size.

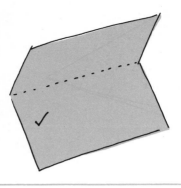

2. Put a pencil check mark on the side of the sheet that is facing up. (This is just to help keep track of which side is which.) Fold the sheet in half. Crease the fold firmly by running a fingernail over it or rubbing it with a spoon. (Do this to all folds as you make them.)

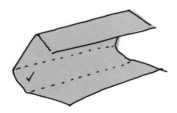

3. Unfold. (The pencil check is still up.) Bring the bottom edge up to the center fold and crease. Then do the same with the top edge.

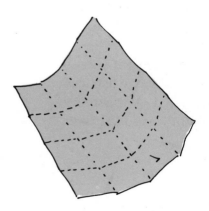

4. Now, without turning the paper over (check side up) repeat the above steps, but from side to side. This will give you sixteen squares.

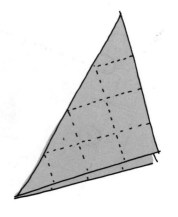

5. Turn the paper over (check side down). Fold the sheet in half along the diagonal. Crease well. Unfold.

6. Repeat this step along the other diagonal.

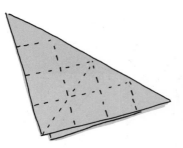

7. With the check side still down, fold each corner to the center. Crease well and unfold.

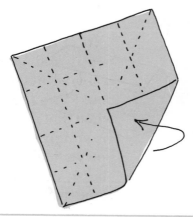

8. Now cut a slit along all four sides of the sheet. They should be as long as one crease.

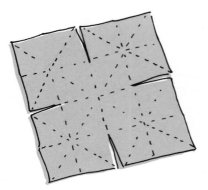

Push up circled places.

9. With the check side still down, put your hand underneath the center of the sheet and push up. This will pop up the center. Do the same with the center point of the other four sections.

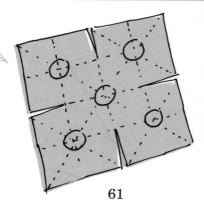

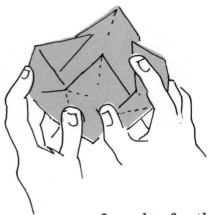

10. Now turn the sheet over (check side up) and gently bunch it together using both hands. The sheet will form itself into a polyhedron.

In order for the polyhedron to hold its shape permanently and firmly, you will have to repeat this entire process and make another polyhedron to fit inside the first one. Place the open side of the second one facing inwards when you fit it inside the first one. Adjust them until they fit snugly together. Then paste down the loose edges. If you've had trouble getting the polyhedron to fall into shape, the chances are you skipped one of the steps. Get some more paper and try again!

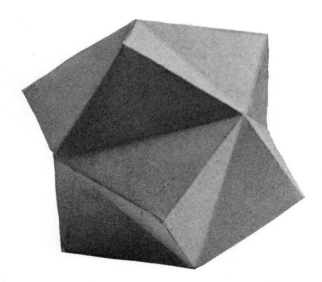

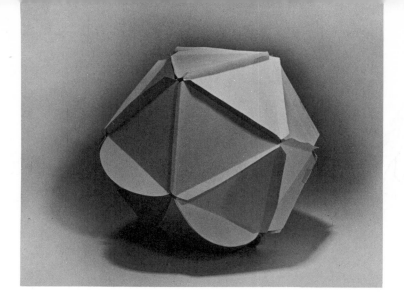

A Globe

This globe is made from a series of circles. You may notice, however, that the actual surface of this form is made up of triangles. The rounded flap, which is bent up, only serves as a means of attachment. In the globe above, part of the rounded flaps have been cut off. Only two have been left on the lower left. Use a strong paper for this project. Construction paper, bristol board or paper of this sort will work best.

1. With a compass draw twenty circles about three or four inches in diameter.

2. Make an equilateral triangle from a piece of cardboard that will just fit into the circle. It is made as shown below.

 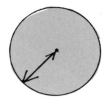 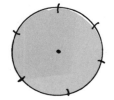 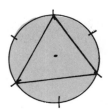

raw a circle with your
ompass the same size as
step number one.

With the compass, measure the distance from the center to the edge of the circle. (This is the radius.) The compass will remain at the same setting as when you drew the circle.

Mark this distance all around the edge (circumference) of the circle.

Connect every other mark and you have a triangle with three equal sides — an equilateral triangle. You can cut it out now and use it as a guide for drawing the triangles in all the circles.

3. Score three lines on each circle using your triangle as a guide. Bend up the three arcs on the sides of the triangle.

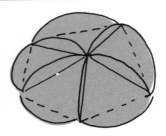

4. Paste together the flaps of five of the circles to form the top of the globe. Repeat this to get the bottom of the globe.

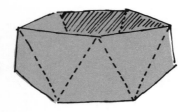

5. Fasten the other ten circles together in a strip. Then form into a circle.

For purposes of clarity, the circles are shown without flaps — in other words, as triangles!

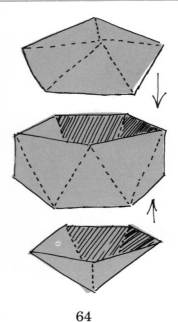

6. The globe is completed by attaching the top and bottom sections to the center one.

A Geodesic Dome

One of the important architectural inventions of this century is the geodesic dome. It was developed by a scientist named Buckminster Fuller. It is a light weight, very strong kind of construction that can enclose large spaces with a minimum of materials. The principle of the dome is that the units of which it is made will direct their thrust and spread their weight evenly to one another. So there is no need for a lot of inside columns and supports.

The globe which is explained on the previous page is very much like a geodesic dome, and you can make one in

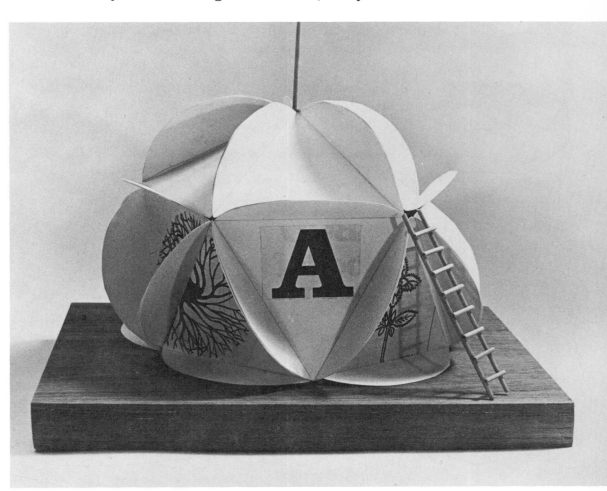

exactly the same way. The only difference is that you will have to eliminate the lower section, and then arrange some means of supporting or finishing off the bottom.

The round flaps which connect the circles can be cut off. You just need a thin edge to connect one triangle to another. (Be sure there is glue along this part.) You may want to add doors and windows to give an air of realism.

Pyramids

The simple, four-sided pyramids illustrated on the opposite page are nice just by themselves, but become particularly interesting when covered with various decorative materials such as photographs, colored and textured papers, and so on. It is also fun to combine them in different ways. The tall combination opposite is held together by a thin stick running right through the three pyramids. A fairly stiff paper should be used to make these shapes.

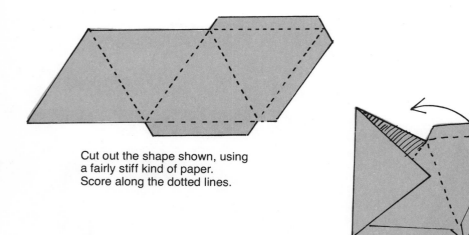

Cut out the shape shown, using a fairly stiff kind of paper. Score along the dotted lines.

Then fold along the dotted lines. Bunch up the edges to get the pyramid. Apply glue to the three tabs, which should be on the inside. Hold together for a minute or two until the glue dries.

66

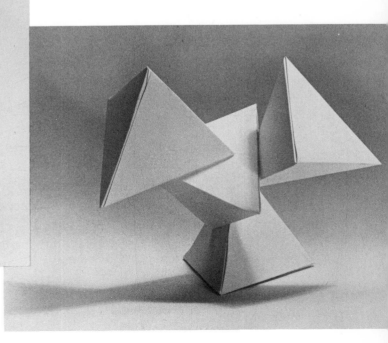

9. HOW TO MAKE YOUR OWN PAPER

Most paper is made today in huge factories that turn it out by the ton — a mile a minute. However, there are also a few skilled and patient craftsmen who produce very high quality paper by hand, a sheet at a time. They do it almost the same way it was done hundreds of years ago. These hand-made papers are used only for special purposes such as expensive, limited-edition books or for etchings and lithographs.

Papers of this sort are made by a very simple process which you can try yourself. The only equipment you need is a piece of window screening and a few items found in every kitchen.

First, you have to make the pulp. This is the raw material of paper. The pulp is made from cellulose fibers, a substance that is stringy, thread-like, pliable. It is found in all plants, and it is the main ingredient in wood. (Half the trees cut down are used not for lumber, but for paper-making.) Other plants that are sometimes used in making paper are cotton plants, rice, wheat and grasses such as hemp, jute and many similar materials.

68

When the cellulose fibers are chopped up and shredded into very fine pieces and mixed with water, we get a soupy mixture which is called pulp. For your first attempt at paper-making get your pulp in a simple, foolproof way by reusing old paper. Get two or three large sheets of blotting paper and a handful of facial or toilet tissue and put these in a bowl with two or three cups of water. If you can't find any blotting paper, use paper towels, some newspaper and facial and toilet tissue.

Mix the pulp thoroughly until you have a thick, even "soup". This mixing is important because if there are lumps and clots you will get weak, uneven paper. An egg-beater is a good tool for beating. An electric beater is even better.

1. When the pulp is an even, smooth mixture, pour it into a deep, rectangular baking pan. Add another cup or two of water until the mixture is like cream, rather than thick soup. Add instant laundry starch in the proportion of one tablespoon to two cups of water.

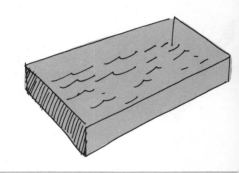

2. Get a piece of window screening about 8 inches by 10 inches. It can be copper, aluminum or plastic. Stir up the pulp. Then slide the screen down into the bottom of the pan and gently lift it up. Keep it flat, without sagging in the center. As you lift it shake it from side to side and front to back so that the fibers cross one another and even out. They should be spread evenly over the screen, not lumped up in the middle.

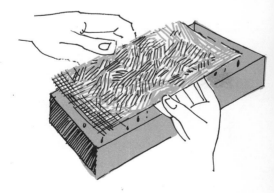

3. Hold the screen with the pulp on it over your pan for a moment while the water drains off.

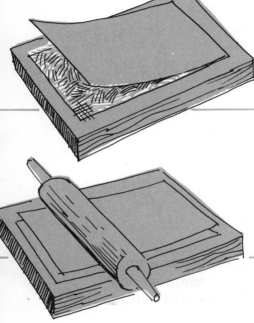

4. Then place it on a flat surface or a board. Place a clean rag on top.

5. Go over the "sandwich" with a rolling pin or a bottle to squeeze out as much water as possible. This is a messy operation so you should work on a board which is placed over a sink.

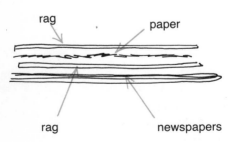

rag   paper

rag   newspapers

6. Now flop the sandwich over onto a pile of newspapers or some towels. Remove the screen. Put another clean rag on top and see if you can squeeze out some more water. Remove the rags carefully. The paper will be very delicate at this point. Put it out in the sun or on a hot radiator to dry. If you are impatient to see the finished product, put the new paper between fresh dry rags and go over it with a hot iron. There will be a lot of water left in the paper even after it has been rolled a few times, so you will have to do quite a bit of ironing and rag changing before the paper is completely dry. Finally, trim the edges with a pair of scissors.

After you've made your first sheet of paper this way you will no doubt want to experiment with other materials in your pulp. The best handmade paper pulp is made from cotton rags. (The best quality paper is called "rag paper.") However it is very difficult to break down and shred the rags into the small cellulose fiber particles that are needed for a good pulp mixture. Special machinery or "beaters" are usually used for this. But you can experiment by cutting up cotton rags with scissors into small pieces and then shredding and chopping them up as best you can with

It is a slow and tedious task grinding up enough old rags or fibrous material in order to get enough pulp to make more than a few sheets of paper.

knife, mallet or between two stones. Add this to a pulp made from blotters and tissue paper. You can also add grasses, threads, banana skins, seaweed and all kinds of fibrous materials.

If you look at a dollar bill through a magnifying glass, you will see very small, thin, red and black fibers scattered about. These help give the paper money a special look which is difficult to copy. Don't try making paper just like this or the FBI is liable to come after you, thinking you are planning to go into the counterfeiting business.

It is surprising the variety of fibers you can find that can be added to the pulp. One day, when I was mixing up a batch of pulp, my dog made the mistake of walking by. After a couple of snips with the scissors, the paper I made that day took on a gray *hairy* look. When you use these various materials in the pulp you must be certain to mix the batch very thoroughly. Remove any lumps or clots of material that won't break down and spread these evenly into the mixture.

If you decide to make paper in any quantity, you can simplify your work by making a support for the screen and a little removable frame to keep the pulp in place as it is lifted out of the pan. Papermakers call the screen a "mould", and the removable frame is called a "deckle".

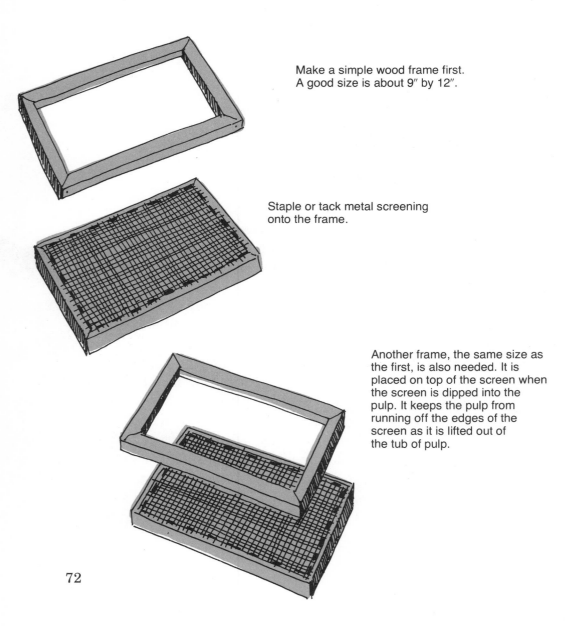

Make a simple wood frame first. A good size is about 9″ by 12″.

Staple or tack metal screening onto the frame.

Another frame, the same size as the first, is also needed. It is placed on top of the screen when the screen is dipped into the pulp. It keeps the pulp from running off the edges of the screen as it is lifted out of the tub of pulp.

72